# Whoopie Pies
# and Family Ties

By "Whoopie Pie" Pam Jarrell

Whoopie Pies and Family Ties
Copyright © 2014 by Pamela Jarrell
All Rights Reserved

Cover Art by:
Chris Mucklow Myer
Memories by Chris

Dedicated to **Walnut Creek Cheese** where I purchased my very first Whoopie Pie and to **Schmidt John Miller**, the one who so aptly named me "Whoopie Pie" Pam.   Not because I make them... but because they are my food obsession.

## Acknowledgements

As a writer, it is never clear which people, places, or events will bring inspiration to us to create a story. A special acknowledgement goes out to my parents for the hands-on introduction to the Amish Culture that I had only had the opportunity to read about. A heartfelt thanks to my children: Seaton, Monica, Samantha and my precious grandchildren Sydney, Logan and Bella for loving me just the way I am. A huge thank you to Sue Laitinen who never complains when I want to "bounce" something off of her. To John and Carolyn Bodine, your unconditional love amazes me. Bonnie, Kay & Tammy... your friendship keeps me going. A special thanks to Miriam Beachy and the staff at Walnut Creek Cheese. You have given me opportunities and memories that will forever be in my heart. To Chris whose photography is beautiful. Last and certainly not least... Bruce and Maggie who give me strength (and coffee) to pick my self up and smile.

**Other Books By Pam Jarrell**

**Whoopie Pie Pam's Kitchen Collection**
Cookie Exchange Party
Home For The Holidays
Delicious Easter Memories
Sizzling Summer Fun
Complete Kitchen Collection

**The Divine Secrets Of The Whoopie Pie Sisters**
Co-Authored with Sarah Price

**Life Regained**
Co-Authored with Sarah Price

**Whoopie Pie Contest Winners**

Congratulations To The Winners Of The
***Walnut Creek Cheese*** Whoopie Pie Contest


Best of All Grand Prize
***Debbie Biddle***
Chocolate Streusel Whoopie Pie


Best Texture, Taste & Appearance
***Dena Schrock***
Cranberry White Chip Whoopie Pie


Most Creative
***Sue Gibson***
Owl Whoopie Pie


A HUGE thank you to all the participants in the contest!

The recipes in this book are from family, friends, participants in the Walnut Creek Whoopie Pie Contest, held on November 7, 2013, and myself. They are presented to you just as they were contributed. Any reference to a particular brand is not an endorsement, just a preferred product by the contributor.

~

What an honor it was for me to have been invited to participate in the Whoopie Pie Contest at Walnut Creek Cheese. It was truly a little piece of heaven on earth being surrounded by all the wonderful people and the different flavorings of my favorite food... Whoopie Pies.

~

This book is formatted in a way that gives you the full recipe and maximum space allowable to make your own notes as you cook each recipe.

# Table of Contents

For I know the thoughts that I think toward you,
saith the Lord, thoughts of peace, and not of evil,
to give you an expected end.
Jeremiah 29:11 (KJV)

## Foreword

I met Pam a few years ago as a customer in our store, Walnut Creek Cheese. From the minute I met her I knew she was not just an average customer, but also a memorable one. Pam, with her effervescent personality, makes a lasting impression on the people who meet her. Smiling, sparkling and fun describes Pam, which explains how she makes new friends so easily.

Pam's smile and love of Whoopie Pies is contagious. Before I met her, Whoopie Pies were simply two cookies with icing between them. But no- she changed all of that for me. The sky is the limit to combinations and flavors according to her love for these cookies. She inspired us here at Walnut Creek Cheese to hold an event planned around the Whoopie Pie. We invited the community to a Whoopie Pie Contest with prizes and fun with Pam as the Guest of Honor. Dozens of Whoopie Pies poured in on the day of the contest and the judges tasted Whoopie Pies till they were literally stuffed with goodness. Keeping Pam out of them proved quite the challenge until the judging was over. But the moment we let her sample the wonderful sweets, she certainly had a smile on her face. Most of the recipes in this book are a result of that memorable day. I'm sure you will enjoy them as much as we did the day of the contest.

Now when I see Whoopie Pies, I always think of Whoopie Pie Pam.

The amazing thing about Pam is her uplifting attitude towards whatever life brings her way. She has faced some incredible challenges and has experienced real miracles that can only be explained as being from God.

She inspires all of us with her faith, stories and books... and most importantly, with her life.

Love you Pam,

Miriam Beachy
Walnut Creek Cheese

### Whoopie Pies and Family Ties

*In one of my college English courses, my professor informed me that I write like I talk. For this story, although there will be editors going through it, I've asked that some things be left "in my voice". That means that all things may not be in proper grammar.*

When it was suggested on several occasions that I write "my" story about being Whoopie Pie Pam, I shrugged it off. "Um, no" was always my answer. And this answer was simply because I felt that my story is no different that anyone else's so why write it? We all, each one of us have a story. Through our daily lives, our families, and being a part of this crazy world, we are given stories to share. For that reason, I began including stories in my cookbooks from the very beginning. I wanted these cookbooks to be unique and personal. Just as the way we each cook. Giving each food item our own flare for taste. I am very blessed, although given many trials, that through each step; I've had God to guide me. I've not always listened but he has never given up on me. Not even today, as I am known as Whoopie Pie Pam and pen books under that name given to me many years ago, do I deserve the grace that God bestows on me. As I dig deep into my mind and heart and begin to write "my" story, I know that I cannot fully tell of all the memories and experiences that have brought me

15

through this life. Nor can I mention all those individuals who are important to me. I also know that somewhere along the way, my children and grandchildren will read this and the message I want them to know is I made mistakes, I faced each battle and I picked myself up, looked towards God, put my big girl panties on and faced life with a smile. Just as each of us does when we open our hearts, I am exposing myself to criticism. But somewhere deep down, that little voice that I believe is God is whispering to me that somewhere, someplace there may be one person whose life is just like mine and by reading this, they will know that they aren't alone in this world... there is someone just as crazy as they are (that would be me) and that this person (me) wants to share with them how God has been her savior, her provider, and her protector from the moment she was born.

~

In the year 2000, my life was in yet another whirlwind. I was in a failing marriage. My second. My first was to my high school sweetheart. A man of high ambition and integrity who came from a family with the same values. Life took its toll on that marriage but from it two beautiful children were born. I can't say that I regret that marriage although it failed. I only regret that it ended and lives were mangled because of it. Mistakes were made that can never be corrected. But, life moved on. I eventually married someone from my teen years

16

that I had met at church camp and had reconnected with. I thought it was fate. From this marriage, my youngest daughter arrived. Giving me three wonderful children. At this point in my life I was working a 50 (plus) hour a week job all the while trying to be a mother, keeping a home and being a wife. In that year on a dark night, I suddenly found myself in an emergency room followed by being in front of a judge asking for a restraining order against my husband. Over the next couple of days I led a life that in my head couldn't be mine. It was only one that you would see on TV. But no, unfortunately, it was mine. I will say that although I am very impressed with the Domestic Violence Division in the city that I was living, it also saddens me that there is such a need for it. I never realized how many people were leading the life that I had only just begun to see. The solution for me was to move back to my hometown, yet still today I worry about those who may not have the support that I had and struggle with abuse daily. In my heart I wish I could encourage everyone facing this to be brave and seek help!

My parents have been married for 53 years. They are truly each other's best friends. They've weathered everything that has been thrown at them over these years. Growing up it was always them against us kids. We knew that, unlike today's children, we couldn't manipulate one parent against the other. Being the oldest child I've seen more than the others have. I was there in the early stages of their marriage. The hard times when young couples struggle to build a life for themselves as a family. I came into the world a little over a year after my parents said, "I do". Sadly, there is only one blurry picture of this happy day for them. As I look at them now, I do it with envy. They managed to accomplish something that is very rare in today's world. They found happiness in their marriage, their home and their lives. God gets all the glory. I've said often that they lead a sheltered life in their little spot in the world setting standards for their happy life that my siblings and I have yet to fully accomplish. My father worked his whole life as a Union Electrician and my mother as a homemaker. We were your typical blue-collar family barely getting by in the 60s and 70s. Our home was in the country and there were days as a young girl that I can remember leaving home in the morning and not returning until lunchtime, which was required so mom would know that I was ok. Can you imagine allowing your children to do that today? Shoot, I knew that if I didn't get out from under my mother's feet she would find a chore for me to do. There was no TV, video games, or computers to occupy us. Being from the hills of Kentucky, we were your typical stereotype family. My paternal grandparents lived on one side of us and my paternal great-grandparents' home was on the other. I wouldn't have wanted to grow up any other way. So many stories that we have to share of those times. These stories will live in our hearts forever.

Faith and God were a strong backbone of my youth.

My paternal great-grandmother was known for her strong beliefs in God. So much so, she started a small church not far from her home. A place where those in the community could attend and worship. My paternal grandmother, her daughter, followed in her footsteps. Not in starting a church but in continuing to follow her God. A belief that she instilled in all of those around her. She raised four children on the belief that God was her savior and would provide. My Grandmother Gladys loved each one of us unconditionally. And that was saying something because there were many times that we didn't deserve it. Living next to her and having a mother whose faith in God was strong as well is the foundation that has brought me to know who God is. Although my life has not always been one that I am proud of and at times I have brought shame to my family and God, I know in my heart that without their faith, I wouldn't be who I am today.

In that same year of 2000, my parents, who love to travel, took me to Ohio Amish Country. There are no words to describe how excited I was to travel and experience the Amish Culture first hand. Up until then, I had only read about them. From the very first book that I read in the 1980s that featured a Mennonite man, I was hooked. I had no clue what being Mennonite or Amish meant. I'm all about reading romance novels. I even named my first child, my son, after one of the heroes in a romance novel by Kathleen Woodiwiss. I still have that book and my son still gets embarrassed when I tell it. On the first day of school one year, he came home all frustrated. He said, "Mom, why did you have to give me this stupid name? My teachers always want to know where you came up with this name. (rolling his eyes) It's embarrassing to tell them you got it out of a trashy novel. Geez mom." He said as he stomped to his room. What can I say? I'm a romantic at heart. From my teen years on, I read every romance novel I could get my hands on. Lisa, one of my dear childhood friend's, mother had every Harlequin book published each month. And she kept them all over the years. I would leave their home with a large brown paper bag full of delicious romantic stories that Ann was allowing me to borrow. She was my library and I blame her for my reading obsession. I'd hibernate for hours. Reading and dreaming of that day that I would meet my prince charming, have 2.5 kids, a white picket fence and live a happily ever after. That's all I wanted. I never dreamed of college or a career outside of the home. And I definitely never dreamed of every writing a book. I still find my escape from reality between the covers of a good romance novel. My genre of choice is Amish Fiction, followed by Christian Fiction and then an occasional trashy novel. Old habits are sometimes hard to break. But by far, I would rather sit down with a good Amish Fiction novel than anything. The culture that will intrigue me until the day I die.

When visiting in Ohio with my parents, they introduced me to an Amish family, The Millers. My parents had become friends with this family through another acquaintance of theirs. My dad and the matriarch of the Miller family, John, became friends, as did my mother and John's Effie. A friendship that my parents still value today although a couple of years ago, John passed away. In the Amish culture, the wife's name always follows her husband's. She's never just Effie. She's John's Effie. They are the John Miller family. I became at awe of this family because of their family values, their hard work and their happiness. Their life appeared to be a simple one and a very inviting one to me. Yes, I romanticized in my head about how easy and simple their life was. This was a life that we "Englishers", as we are referred to by the Amish, only dream of having. It was only later on in life that I realized their life wasn't the simple one that I had first thought it was.

From that first visit to today, visiting the Ohio Amish is a vital part of my world. Now it's as though I am traveling home instead of on vacation. What began as a trip with my parents turned into an annual "Housewives' Sabbatical" for myself and five other ladies. Each year I would travel with my mom, Gail, Daisy, Denise and my sister Tina, to Ohio Amish country for a week long vacation of no laundry, no cooking, no cleaning and no phones. We would travel through the countryside and shop during the day and when the sidewalks rolled up at 5pm, we would retreat to our townhouse, sit on the porch and read. Never tiring of hearing and seeing an Amish buggy as it clip-clopped by. All the while, straining to get a glimpse of its passengers in their black attire. Wondering where they were heading. Of course, while sitting on the porch of this townhouse, we were reading Amish fiction. These women were just as passionate about Amish fiction novels as I was. My mother, who was never a reader, now reads more than I did. Wait... what? My mom reads? The woman who used to tell me that I read too much? I loved it. And I never missed a moment to remind her of this. I still don't. Back then; Amish Fiction books weren't in abundance as they are today. They were scarce. Beverly Lewis was our first Amish Fiction author. And for a while, she was our only one. I wonder if she realizes how her talent has touched so many lives? And if she does realize it, how has she remained the humble lady that I had the privilege to spend some time with last year? When reading her books back then the farthest thing from my mind was that I would ever have the honor of being in communication with her. Hey... the day I met her ranks right up there with my dream of meeting Elvis. (Which never happened) That's saying something because I, like a million other women, drooled over Elvis. From reading Beverly Lewis' books, along came Dale Cramer and Wanda Brunstetter novels. And I was hooked on them as well. I bought every book that I could find and for years, had my own library in my home. I took great pride in that little library. I am excited that in this past year I was able to meet both Dale Cramer and Wanda Brunstetter as well as Wanda's husband Richard. To be amongst such talent was a blessing. Oh if I knew how to get

22

that talent to rub off on me...

The years to follow 2000 became one of a roller coaster ride with many ups and downs. Trying to find my way in this crazy thing we call life. Making mistakes. Trying to better myself but not always succeeding. In and out of a couple of relationships yet never finding that little piece of happiness that I read in those romance novels. Wondering where I had gone wrong because I didn't get that white picket fence with those 2.5 children who respected me and a husband who loved me. I was taking life one day at a time. My love for Amish fiction and the Amish culture grew with each year as did my love for God. After what I consider the biggest mistake of my life and a mini-stroke, topped with a relationship that had betrayed me I realized that the only thing I wanted in life was health & happiness for my children, who had suffered through all my mistakes, and for me to find out who Pam really was in God's world. By this time, God had blessed me with two precious grand children. The moment that I looked in each of my children's eyes after they were born is priceless and nothing can ever be more than that with the exception of holding those grandchildren and looking into their little faces. Moments that warm your heart like nothing else can.

My journey to know more about God began. Most of my life I had heard sermons on hell, fire & damnation and I understood God to be a punishing God. Imagine my surprise when I first heard that he was a loving God full of compassion.

Was this true? I wanted to know more. During this time I felt the urge to go to my church. I had been in attendance at Christ Temple Church in Huntington, WV. for a couple of years and was faithful in my attendance but this particular day was during the day hours. Upon arrival at the church, I asked if there was anything I could do. Before receiving an answer, I decided to clean the front glass doors. I went in search of glass cleaner and a rag. For 10 minutes, I searched that closet for glass cleaner. I knew it had to be there but it wasn't. I finally gave up and asked a lady who was passing by if she seen it. Sure enough... it was right in front of me. As she handed me the glass cleaner, she paused. What came out of her mouth at that point was, "You need God now more than ever. You're lost." That statement began what I refer to as a snot-fest right there in that closet. From there it moved across the hall to the bathroom, which was the ladies original destination, to wash our faces and blow our noses. It continued on for another hour. I have referred to this lady as my Spiritual Closet mom since that day. There is no doubt in my mind that God used her over the next several years to hold my hand and guide me down a spiritual path for a better understanding as to who Pam is in God's world. Odd how strangers come into our lives and we fully listen to them when at times we won't even listen to our own families. God truly brought me through this horrible time of my life and my love affair with him fully began.

Throughout the next few years my focus was on God, my family and myself. Dating was not an option. I wouldn't entertain that there was a prince charming anywhere on this earth. Sadly I still don't. We teach our young girls these fairy tales when in reality; no man can live up to that. Only God can. After my failed marriages and a deep relationship, I had no desire to open my heart for anyone else. I wasn't bitter. I was just realistic. My life, although not what I had wanted it to be was full. My family was healthy, what more could I ask for. At that point I was following God's will for me and if God wanted me to have another man in my life then he would have to run me over in church with him because that's the only place he was going to find me. That day came several years later when a man who I had never met, yet had been in the same church and sat in the same area as I had for two years, ran over my foot in the Narthex of our church with his motorcycle as he was pushing it out. You really have to watch what you say or ask for because God really does listen and tries to give us the desires of our hearts. Later on, that man became my husband.

In 2010, while preparing to leave out of town that evening for a short trip with friends, I began feeling odd. I went to the Dr. and they immediately loaded me into an ambulance. I was having what they thought was a stroke. Turns out they labeled it a mini-stroke. I was released from the hospital the next day and continued, feeling fine, onto our mini vacation. The following week I began feeling odd again while on a phone conversation with my daughter. I lost my speech and the use of my right side. Again, I was loaded into an ambulance with the signs of a stroke. I was hospitalized for a week and had every test possible that had initials (MRI, CAT, etc). The diagnosis was hemiplegic migraines. The aura of these migraines presents themselves initially with the same signs of a stroke. With the exception that the hemiplegic migraine ones go away after a period of time. During this week long stay, a Dr. who works in the hospital, Dr. Johnson, came to my hospital room and over the next hour she explained to me that there was something in the area of my thyroid that caused her concern and although that was not why I was in the hospital, she asked if she could look into it further. Because of her findings, I found out that I had nodules in my thyroid area. I had a full thyroidectomy and the nodules removed. From there, the biopsy on these nodules was good however the cells behind my thyroid were cancerous. I was diagnosed with Papillary Thyroid Carcinoma. For the next three years of my life, I received not just that diagnosis but I received it again. Resulting in two rounds of radiation and other treatments, diets, etc. I felt as though I was drained. I became a couch potato. My body rebelled in any way it could to make daily life hard. During this time, although my body did not work, my mind still did. Being an active lively individual, going to a sedimentary state brings more emotions to your soul than you ever thought existed. I felt that I was nothing. Worthless. Useless. Although I knew there were others out there so much

26

worse off than me, it didn't take away my pain. As I went to each Dr. Appointment, and each treatment, I did so by myself. As I heard each diagnosis and the ugly C word, I was alone. My children were grown with hectic lives of their own and I didn't expect them to be there. The husband that God had sent me was working and couldn't take off. I was thankful that he provided a roof over my head and the medical insurance that I needed for these treatments but my heart felt lonely. I never fully understood why he couldn't take vacation time and accompany me to these appointments. As I look back now, I realize, that was a huge factor in my marriage eventually ending. On the third diagnosis of cancer, I was told it had now spread to my lymph nodes. Again, another round of tests were ran. Unlike the first two times, I was not settled in my soul with this diagnosis. I was struggling to face this one as I had the other two with a smile on my face and optimistic. I was troubled. I was informed at the Dr.'s office that I was scheduled for surgery in February. They were going to go in and clean out my lymph nodes. That meant I would have a scar from one side of my head to the other along my upper neckline. From there an aggressive round of chemo would follow. Radiation had made me sick so I could only imagine what chemo would do to me. Knowing this was ahead of me and the fact that I had not traveled to Amish country for over a year, I knew it was time. I knew I needed to make that journey. I've always found peace for my soul in Ohio Amish country. There and the ocean are my two places of peace. I can sit on the beach watching the waves crash against the shore and get more peace in ten minutes than I can a whole day somewhere else. At this time, I was being drawn to Ohio. Accompanied by Gail, one of the original "Housewives' Sabbatical" ladies, we left. When I am in Amish country, rarely does my cell phone work. This trip was no different. Upon arriving in Ohio, we were greeted with snow. This was in January but for me it was unexpected. I don't like snow except for one big one for the winter season and then I'm done. I definitely don't like cold so having both on this trip did not make me happy. But, deep down, I wasn't happy anyway so it really didn't matter. One thing that I was totally surprised about was the amount of Amish people out on the road. They were going down the road in their buggies, on bicycles or walking. In the snow and cold. More than I had ever seen out and about at any given time. One morning I wanted to take a drive in the country. Gail, being slower at rising in the morning than me, stayed behind in the hotel room. As I was driving and admiring the scenery, I seen a pond that had a small boat in the middle of it surrounded by ice. Nothing special but I felt compelled to pull over. As I sat and looked at this little boat stuck out in that pond, unable to go back to shore, I began to pray. Asking God to help ease my unsettled soul. At that moment, I realized that what I was going through was all God's will. Just as I had learned from the Amish, to follow God's will. Why had I forgotten that? Possibly, I was going through all of this because somewhere I would encounter someone, perhaps a member of the medical team that would be treating me that needed to know who my God was and it was going to be my responsibility to tell him or her. I was elated. God was going to use me. I was suddenly okay with the fact that I once again had cancer. My soul was at rest. With a smile in my heart, I drove back to the hotel. My step was a little lighter. By this time, Gail was up and ready to go out. After a little shopping, we both had the desire to drive through the countryside once again. Any time you visit Amish country, these drives are always a learning experience. On this particular drive, I traveled from Mt. Hope to Berlin. The roads were littered with Amish buggies as well as huge semi-trucks that to me were moving too fast and needed to slow down. Out of nowhere, my cell phone rang. My car had the built in hands-free capability so when it rang it startled me. Especially since my phone never worked in that area. Looking at my screen I seen it was my Doctor's office. I had had a round of testing that prior week and I assumed they were calling to tell me something else was wrong. I immediately pulled to the side of the road for fear I would lose signal and miss the call. Calling my Doctor's office back was always impossible. In the years I had been there, I had never been able to call them and actually speak to the person I needed. I always had to leave a message. Imagine my surprise when I answered the phone and it was the Doctor himself. He had never called me so when I heard his voice I knew it was not going to be good. As I listened to his words, tears came to my eyes. I was speechless. Gail could not hear the

29

conversation because I had transferred the call from my car to my actual phone. What Gail could see and hear though was the tears running down my face and all the semi trucks soaring past us as well as the fact that I had pulled over and was in the buggy lane and we had just topped over a hill. Basically, we were sitting ducks in the road. I can't begin to tell you every word that my Doctor spoke but I can tell you that he said the word, "*perplexed*" a lot. He was perplexed. I will hear his foreign voice say that word for the rest of my life. For you see, all the recent tests showed no cancer. No cancer! He was so "*perplexed*" that he consulted with two other doctors before calling me. My surgery, the chemo and all the rest of the medical procedures had been cancelled. He had no answer as to why all these results were clear. But I knew. I knew that I had been prayed over and my God is a God of miracles. And I was witnessing one. To say that God tests us, I can't because I don't know for sure. What I do know is that I felt as though I was and until I became at peace at what I realized was God's will, I couldn't move forward. Now I could. It never ceases to amaze me as to the path we journey on when we give in and follow God's will. But, as human as I am and although I know that I am to give into him daily and follow his will, I still have times I want to do it Pam's way. That's never good.

During the first round of cancer and radiation, to pass time one evening, I made a list of any Amish fiction books that I could find on the Internet. I took that list and created a spreadsheet and within it I listed the title, author and the sequence these books should be read in if they were in a series. (Truth be known, I created this list so my mother would stop asking me which book she was to read in a series. But don't tell her that!) After a restless painful night, I walked into our kitchen for a cup of coffee and to take my daily regimen of medicines. My husband had already gone to work so it was just me, my faithful companions Sophia & Molly, (my Maltese and my daughter's Chihuahua). At that moment, while looking out our kitchen window, wishing I felt like going out into the sun and taking Sophia for a walk, I have no doubt that God spoke gently to my mind. I didn't realize it at first that what I was thinking was from God, because what lay on my mind was to start a Facebook group. A group that I could share my "Big Ole Booklist" (as I had named it) with others who loved Amish fiction as much as I did. I knew nothing about Facebook other than it was for college students and there were not a lot of good things said about it. But, with my physical body in rebellion against everything that my mind wanted it to do, I used my sedimentary state that day and learned all I could about Facebook. Before nightfall, I had created the Whoopie Pie Book Club. As I had mentioned earlier, prior to cancer, we had our "Housewives' Sabbatical". One evening, during one of those trips, as we sat reading and we were eating the Whoopie Pies that I had gotten earlier that day, I jokingly started calling us The Whoopie Pie Book Club so, when creating the Facebook group, I felt that was the most appropriate name for it. I was

31

after all, Whoopie Pie Pam.

Many often ask how I came to be known as Whoopie Pie Pam. During one of the "Housewives' Sabbaticals", while shopping at Walnut Creek Cheese, a store that I love in Holmes County, I saw a package of devil's food Whoopie Pies. I was drawn to them so I had to buy the package. It was as though there was a little voice coming from that package that said, "Take me. Eat me. You will love me and I will change your life." That was my first encounter of the dessert that soon became an obsession with me. I truly love Whoopie Pies and anyone who really knows me knows that I don't normally share them. I missed the "sharing your Whoopie Pie" part of Kindergarten. I did however make an exception of sharing them with the Miller Family. As we would visit, I would usually take Whoopie Pies along with me. Did I mention that Whoopie Pies are an obsession? Some people smoke, drink or do drugs... I eat Whoopie Pies. On one of those visits, John laughed and told me that every time he seen me, I had Whoopie Pies and if I didn't watch out I was going to turn into one or get real fat. I haven't turned into one yet and as for the fat part, we'll not discuss that. From that moment on, John called me Whoopie Pie Pam.

When the opportunity arose for me to author a cookbook, I did so using the Whoopie Pie Pam name. It's one that when I hear it, it brings fond memories to me. In November 2012, John passed away. That's the same month and year that my first cookbook was published.

In 2013, my life began to come alive again. My cancer battle was over and my body was rebuilding. Needing out of the house, I began traveling more to Amish country. Through those travels, I have met some wonderful Amish people whom I think of as family. They have opened their hearts and homes to me. I cannot begin to tell you how much I cherish these friends and all that I have learned from them. One lesson I can share though is I've learned to lead a simpler life and to cherish what God has given me. In September 2013, I traveled to Ohio and was joined by several members of The Whoopie Pie Book Club. That was a weekend I will never forget. What bonding began on Facebook was deeply enriched in Holmes County, Ohio. I still humbly shake my head and wonder why these people would spend their hard earned money and take their precious time to travel the distance they did just to spend a weekend with me. I am simply a woman, who's made a lot of mistakes in life but is blessed to have been forgiven by a God who sent his son to die on the cross for my sins. From that gathering, I was invited by Walnut Creek Cheese to attend their Whoopie Pie Contest. That was so much fun! The fellowship was by far a whole lot better than all those Whoopie Pies that I drooled over. From there, I was invited by Hershey Farms to participate in their annual Whoopie Pie Festival. In the beginning of the WPBC (Whoopie Pie Book Club) there were only a handful of members. Today there is approximately 2400 (and growing daily). It's my wish that each of these members knows how thankful I am for them. I had no clue when I obeyed God and founded WPBC that it would lead me to where I am today... known throughout as Whoopie Pie Pam. Interacting with the authors whose works I have so admired. Being a part of the daily lives of my cherished WPBC members. Through this book club, I have formed friendships that are very important to me. These friendships are a huge part of my life. Sue Laitinen is one of them. She keeps me grounded on the days that I want to fly. In 2012, through an incident with another author, I met Sarah Price. Over time we became good friends and today, we share two joint ventures in writing. *The Divine Secrets of The Whoopie Pie Sisters* and *Life Regained*. I have what I refer to as my "Whoopie Pie Sisters". I am the oldest and the one they all talk to when they have problems. During a conversation between us, they were picking at me (as they often do). I informed them that if they didn't stop, I was going to write a book and tell all of their secrets. Two of them instantly began backtracking but not Sarah. Her response was, "YES! Do it! I'll do it with you!" That's how the *Divine Secrets of the Whoopie Pie Sisters* book became into existence. I had a blast writing with Sarah on this book. I never dreamed that it would be as successful as it has been. Within a week of it's release, I was on my way to church when I received a phone call from Sarah. She wanted to know if I was on Amazon. I explained to her that I was on my way to church and wouldn't be on the Internet till the service was over. (Okay, confession... I sometimes get on my phone during church. Sshhh, don't tell the pastor!) What she said to me at that point took a while to register in my pea-sized brain. Our book was ranked at #36 in ALL of Kindle (over millions). I had to ask, "So, you are telling me that at this moment in time, there are only 35 other kindle books selling better than ours?" Her response was "Yes!" I heard nothing else for a little while. I was in shock. Wow... God was blessing our little writing adventure! This day and the day that I was ranked as one of Amazon's Best Selling Authors are days that still seem surreal to me. I'm just a simple country girl... thank you God for your blessings! *Life Regained* came about because I wanted to emphasize on a friendship between an English woman and an Amish one. A friendship, despite their cultural differences, changes their lives. I have three of these friendships that are close to my heart. Marlene, Naomi and Ella are women who I admire deeply. Their strength in life amazes me. I've learned so much from these amazing women. People think I wrote Life Regained after my divorce however it was written way before I even knew that the divorce word would be mentioned again in my life. The extra story line that Sarah added was wonderful and made the book complete. I'm asked often about Carl. Oh yes... Carl. The man in my dreams who became a character in "Life Regained". The man I probably conjured up in my subconscious back when I was reading all the romance novels. The day my mother read *Life Regained*, she sent me a text asking me if I had a "Carl" in Florida and was that my reason for moving. I didn't and it wasn't. But it made me feel good that the book was good enough for her to think that he truly existed. When my life changed with the sudden end of my marriage, I realized that my children were grown and did not need me on a daily basis, my parents were healthy and I was single. The previous winter months were harsh in West Virginia and I wasn't sure I could withstand another one. I boarded a plane to travel to Florida for a visit with two dear friends, John and Carolyn. Through that visit, I realized that God was directing me to Florida. And here I am. I've met new friends, I've grown in my faith and my life is moving on. Granted, I am not the same person I was in January 2014, but I hope that with God's guidance I will be a better one. I've just returned home from a trip to Pennsylvania where I was privileged to be a part of Hershey Farm's Whoopie Pie Festival. I invited along with me four other authors to share this experience with me. The day before the festival, I boarded a tour bus to spend the day with some of my cherished members of the Whoppie Pie Book Club. Despite some obstacles, we had a fabulous time and just as the gathering in 2013, we formed a lifetime bond.

Although the year 2014 began like a tornado and once again, the rug was pulled out from under me and I was forced to make changes in my life, I cannot tell you that it's been a bad year. But it's been a year of taking the old Whoopie Pie Pam and making a new one. While things were falling apart in my life, they are also falling together. I have no clue as to the destination that God is leading me. I may never know. But the one thing that I am certain of is that God does love me and I love my members of Whoopie Pie Book Club. I am not in a season that allows me to travel to Amish country as often as I was used to so I miss them dearly. They are such a huge part of my life. But as stated in Ecclesiastes... To everything there is a season. As my seasons change: I will adapt. I will make mistakes. I will continue to strengthen my faith and follow a mighty loving God wherever he leads me and I will be... Whoopie Pie Pam, living the second part of her story and giving all she has to serving him.

Blessings to each of you as your own story unfolds,

*"Whoopie Pie" Pam*

**Ecclesiastes 8:1-8 (KJV)**

*To every thing there is a season, and a time to every*
*purpose under the heaven:*

*A time to be born, and a time to die;*

*A time to plant, and a time to pluck up that which is*
*planted;*

*A time to kill, and a time to heal; a time to break down,*
*and a time to build up;*

*A time to weep, and a time to laugh; a time to mourn,*
*and a time to dance;*

*A time to cast away stones,*
*and a time to gather stones together;*

*A time to embrace, and a time to refrain from*
*embracing;*

*A time to get, and a time to lose; a time to keep,*
*and a time to cast away;*

*A time to rend, and a time to sew; a time to keep silence,*
*and a time to speak;*

*A time to love, and a time to hate; a time of war,*
*and a time of peace.*

## Whoopie Pie Pam's FAVORITE

*Chocolate Strawberry Shortcake Whoopie Pies*

1 pkg. (2-layer size) chocolate cake mix
3/4 cup water
1/2 cup oil
3 eggs
1 pkg. (8 oz.) PHILADELPHIA Cream Cheese, softened
1 jar (7 oz.) JET-PUFFED Marshmallow Creme
1 tub (8 oz.) COOL WHIP Whipped Topping, thawed
3 cups fresh strawberries, sliced

**HEAT** oven to 350ºF.
**BEAT** first 4 ingredients with mixer until well blended. Drop 2 Tbsp. batter, 2 inches apart, into 32 mounds on baking sheets sprayed with cooking spray.
**BAKE** 10 min. or until toothpick inserted in centers comes out almost clean. Cool on baking sheets 3 min. Remove to wire racks; cool completely.
**BEAT** cream cheese and marshmallow creme in large bowl with mixer until well blended. Add COOL WHIP; beat on low speed just until blended.
**SPREAD** about 2 Tbsp. COOL WHIP mixture onto bottom side of each of 16 cookies. Top with strawberries and remaining cookies.

## Apple Spice Whoopie Pie

*Contest Entry of Elizabeth Young*

- ½ cup butter, softened
- 1 ¼ cups brown sugar, packed
- 1 teaspoon baking soda
- 1 teaspoon apple pie spice
- ¼ teaspoon salt
- 1 egg
- ¼ cup applesauce
- ¼ cup half and half
- 2 ½ cups of "Sapphire" flour
- 1 large Mutsu apple, peeled and grated (approximately 1 cup)

Preheat oven to 350° F.
Cover baking sheets with parchment paper, set aside.
In the bowl of a stand mixer fitted with the paddle attachment, add butter and beat on medium speed until creamy (about 30 seconds).
Add in brown sugar, baking soda, apple pie spice & salt. Pulse until well incorporated.
Add egg and pulse until combined.
Add in applesauce & half and half and mix on low speed until fully incorporated.
Add in flour a little at a time and mix until combined.
Add apple and fold into mixture with spatula. Pipe dough onto prepared baking sheets approximately 2 inches apart.
Bake for 10 minutes until tops are lightly browned.
Let stand a couple minutes on cookie sheets to set and then transfer to cooling rack to cool completely.

*Fill with Apple Spice Filling

**Apple Spice Filling**

- 8 tablespoons butter, softened
- ¼ cup of powdered sugar
- 1/3 cup of ricotta cheese
- 1 teaspoon honey

Beat the butter until light and airy.
Add the powdered sugar and beat until creamy.
Add the ricotta and honey: beat for 1 minute.
Scrape down the bowl and beat for 2 to 3 minutes until the filling is light and fluffy.
Spread cheese filling on bottom half of cookies and top with remaining half of cookies.
Press together. Store in refrigerator.

## Caramel Apple Whoopie Pies

*Contest Entry of Teresa Young*

- 1/2 cup butter, softened
- 1 1/4 cups brown sugar, packed
- 1 teaspoon baking soda
- 1 teaspoon apple pie spice
- 1/4 teaspoon salt
- 1 egg
- 1/4 cup applesauce
- 1/4 cup half and half
- 2 1/2 cups of "Sapphire" flour
- 1 large Mutsu apple, peeled and grated (approximately 1 cup)

Preheat oven to 350° F.
Cover baking sheets with parchment paper, set aside.
In the bowl of a stand mixer fitted with the paddle attachment, add butter and beat on medium speed until creamy (about 30 seconds).
Add in brown sugar, baking soda, apple pie spice & salt. Pulse until well incorporated.
Add egg and pulse until combined.
Add in applesauce & half and half and mix on low speed until fully incorporated.
Add in flour a little at a time and mix until combined.
Add apple and fold into mixture with spatula.
Pipe dough onto prepared baking sheets approximately 2 inches apart.
Bake for 10 minutes until tops are lightly browned.
Let stand a couple minutes on cookie sheets to set and then transfer to cooling rack to cool completely.

*Fill with Caramel Apple Filling

**Caramel Apple Filling**

- 4 ounces mascarpone cheese, at room temperature
- 3 ounces cream cheese, at room temperature
- 1/3 cup powdered sugar
- 14 caramel melting candies
- 1/8 cup of half and half

Beat together the mascarpone and cream cheese, about 3 minutes.
Add sugar and beat.
Melt the caramel candies and half and half over a stovetop.
Beat into the cheese mixture for another 2 minutes.
Spread cheese filling on bottom half of cookies and top with remaining half of cookies and press together.
Store in refrigerator.

## Caramel Chocolate Coffee Whoopie Pies

*Contest Entry of Danielle Feldner*

- 2 1/4 cups flour
- 1 teaspoon baking soda
- 1/2 teaspoon baking powder
- 1/2 teaspoon salt
- 1 cup sugar
- 1/2 cup vegetable oil
- 1 large egg
- 1/2 teaspoon caramel flavor concentrate
- 1/2 teaspoon vanilla
- 1/2 cup yogurt
- 1/2 cup plus 2 tablespoons hot strong coffee
- 1/3 cup cocoa powder

Preheat oven to 350° F and grease several baking sheets.
Sift together flour, soda, baking powder and salt.
In another bowl beat sugar and shortening until fluffy, then add egg and caramel and vanilla extracts and blend thoroughly.
Add half of flour mixture with half the yogurt and half the yogurt and half the coffee. Repeat with the remaining halves beating until light and smooth.
In another bowl mix 1 cup batter with 1/3 cup cocoa powder and 2 tablespoons coffee.
Scoop about 3/4 tablespoons chocolate batter onto cookie sheets 2 inches apart.
Scoop original batter, about a tablespoon, onto chocolate batter and swirl with toothpick.
Bake about 10 minutes and cool.  Makes 14 Whoopie Pies

*Fill with Caramel Chocolate Coffee Filling

44

### Caramel Chocolate Coffee Filling

- 1/2 cup butter
- 1/4 cup vegetable shortening
- 1 1/2 cup powdered sugar
- 3 tablespoons marshmallow fluff
- 1 egg white
- 1/2 teaspoon caramel flavor concentrate
- 1/2 teaspoon vanilla extract
- Pinch of salt
- 1/4 cup chopped caramel bits

Combine butter, shortening, powdered sugar, marshmallow fluff, egg white, caramel and vanilla extracts and salt.
Beat till smooth. Fold in chopped caramel.
Spread half the cookie bottoms with filling and sandwich with another cookie.

**Cherry Almond Whoopie Pies**

*Contest Entry of Danielle Feldner*

- 2 1/4 cups flour
- 1 teaspoon baking soda
- 1/2 teaspoon baking powder
- 1/2 teaspoon salt
- 1 cup sugar
- 1/2 cup vegetable shortening
- 1 large egg
- 1/2 teaspoon cherry extract
- 1/2 teaspoon almond extract
- 1/2 cup yogurt
- 1/2 cup hot tea or coffee
- 10 drops red food coloring
- 1/2 cup chopped maraschino cherries

Preheat oven to 350° F and grease several baking sheets.
Sift together flour, baking soda and salt.
In another bowl beat sugar and shortening until fluffy, then add egg and cherry and almond extracts and blend thoroughly
Add half of flour mixture with half of yogurt and half of tea.
Repeat with the remaining halves beating until smooth.
Scoop onto pans with a medium (1 1/2) cookie scoop about 2 inches apart.
Bake cookies for about 10 minutes. Cool on racks.


*Fill with Cherry Almond Filling

46

## Cherry Almond Filling

- 1/2 cup butter
- 1/4 cup vegetable shortening
- 1 1/2 cups powdered sugar or more if need
- 3 tablespoons marshmallow fluff
- 1 egg white
- 1 teaspoon almond extract
- Pinch of salt

Combine butter, shortening, powdered sugar, marshmallow fluff, egg white, almond extract and salt. Beat until light and smooth.
Spread half the cookie bottoms with filling and sandwich with another cookie.

### Chocolate Crinkles

*Contest Entry of Emma Mae Miller*

- 2 cups brown sugar
- 1/2 cup vegetable oil
- 4 eggs
- 2 teaspoons vanilla
- 1/2 cup cocoa
- 2 teaspoons baking powder
- 1/2 teaspoon salt
- 21/4 cups flour
- 1 small box instant chocolate pudding

Mix together in order given.
Chill at least 3 hours.
Roll in powdered sugar and bake at 350° F.
Do not over bake.

*Fill with Chocolate Crinkle Filling

**Chocolate Crinkle Filling**

- 3/4 cup shortening
- 3 cups powdered sugar
- 3/4 cup plus 2 tablespoons marshmallow topping
- 3 tablespoons milk or to spreading consistency
- 1 teaspoon vanilla

Mix all ingredients.
Spread filling on half of the cookies and sandwich with the remaining cookies.

### Chocolate Mint Whoopie Pies

*Contest Entry of Esta Borntrager*

- 2 cups vegetable oil
- 4 cups brown sugar
- 8 eggs
- 2 cups milk
- 2 cups cocoa
- 4 teaspoons soda
- 2 teaspoons salt
- 4 teaspoons vanilla
- 6 cups flour

Mix vegetable oil, brown sugar and eggs till well mixed.
Add cocoa, soda, salt & vanilla and mix well.
Stir in flour alternately with milk using flour last.
Bake at 350° F.

*Fill with Chocolate Mint Filling

### Chocolate Mint Filling

- 1 1/4 cups milk
- 5 tablespoons flour
- pinch of salt.

Boil ingredients until thick.  Cool.

Part 2

- 1 cup Crisco
- 1/2 cup butter
- 1 cup sugar
- 1 teaspoon vanilla
- Andes Mints candies, crushed

Beat together Crisco and butter till creamy.
Add sugar and beat again.
Then add part one and beat till light and fluffy.
Add in Andes Mint candies. Mix well.

### Chocolate Mocha Whoopie Pies

*Contest Entry of Esta Borntrager*

- 2 cups vegetable oil
- 4 cups brown sugar
- 8 eggs
- 2 cups milk
- 2 cups cocoa
- 4 teaspoons soda
- 2 teaspoons salt
- 4 teaspoons vanilla
- 6 cups flour

Mix vegetable oil, brown sugar and eggs till well mixed.
Add cocoa, soda, salt & vanilla and mix well.
Stir in flour alternately with milk using flour last.
Bake at 350° F.

*Fill with Chocolate Mocha Filling

### Chocolate Mocha Filling

- Whip and Ice
- 2 teaspoons instant coffee
- 2 tablespoons hot water
- Mocha Whip Dip
- Snickers Candy Bar, cut up

Beat the Whip and Ice till stiff.
Mix instant coffee with hot water.
Cool and add to Whip and Ice.
Add enough mocha whip dip for the right consistency.
Mix to your taste. Add Snicker bars cut up.

## Chocolate Oreo Whoopie Pies

*Contest Entry of Esta Borntrager*

- 2 cups vegetable oil
- 4 cups brown sugar
- 8 eggs
- 2 cups milk
- 2 cups cocoa
- 4 teaspoons soda
- 2 teaspoons salt
- 4 teaspoons vanilla
- 6 cups flour

Mix vegetable oil, brown sugar and eggs till well mixed.
Add cocoa, soda, salt & vanilla and mix well.
Stir in flour alternately with milk using flour last.
Bake at 350° F.

*Fill with Chocolate Oreo Filling

### Chocolate Oreo Filling

- 1 1/4 cups milk
- 5 tablespoons flour
- pinch of salt.

Boil ingredients until thick.   Cool.

Part 2
- 1 cup Crisco
- 1/2 cup butter
- 1 cup sugar
- 1 teaspoon vanilla
- Oreo cookies, crushed

Beat together Crisco and butter till creamy.
Add sugar and beat again.
Then add part one and beat till light and fluffy.
Add in Oreo Cookies.

## Chocolate Streusel Whoopie pies

*Best Of All Grand Prize Winner ~*
*Contest Entry of Debbie Biddle*

- 1 box of any white cake mix
- 1 small box instant vanilla pudding
- 1 small box instant chocolate fudge pudding mix
- 4 large eggs
- 1 cup water
- 1/2 plus 1 tablespoon oil

Streusel Topping

- 1 cup brown sugar
- 1 cup chopped pecans
- 1 tablespoon cinnamon ( optional )

Preheat oven to 350° F.
Spray Whoopie Pie pan with baking spray.
Mix all cake ingredients until well blended about 2 minutes.
Fill cups about half full and bake 10 minutes.
While those are baking mix the streusel ingredients and sprinkle in another dry Whoopie Pie pan.
When cakes are done immediately remove from pans and lightly spray the tops with spray margarine and insert them top side down on the streusel topping in second pan, immediately return to the oven for an additional minute or two.
Remove from oven and leave in pan to give the streusel topping time to set.
This recipe will make 16-20 Whoopie Pies.

*Fill with Chocolate Streusel Filling

### Chocolate Streusel Filling

- 1/2 cup soft butter
- 1/2 cup shortening
- 2 cups sifted powdered sugar
- 7 1/2 ounces marshmallow fluff
- 1 teaspoon vanilla
- 1/4 teaspoon cinnamon (optional)

In mixer bowl cream together the butter, shortening
and powdered sugar until fluffy.
Add marshmallow fluff and seasonings.
Fill cooled Whoopie pies and refrigerate.

**Chocolate Whoopie Pies**

*Contest Entry of Esta Borntrager*

- 2 cups vegetable oil
- 4 cups brown sugar
- 8 eggs
- 2 cups milk
- 2 cups cocoa
- 4 teaspoons soda
- 2 teaspoons salt
- 4 teaspoons vanilla
- 6 cups flour

Mix vegetable oil, brown sugar and eggs till well mixed.
Add cocoa, soda, salt & vanilla and mix well.
Stir in flour alternately with milk using flour last.
Bake at 350° F.

*Fill with Vanilla Filling

### Vanilla Filling

- 1 1/4 cups milk
- 5 tablespoons flour
- pinch of salt.

Boil ingredients until thick.   Cool.

Part 2
- 1 cup Crisco
- 1/2 cup butter
- 1 cup sugar
- 1 teaspoon vanilla

Beat together Crisco and butter till creamy.
Add sugar and beat again.
Then add part one and beat till light and fluffy.

**My Miracle Mom by Susan Conceicao**

I am the second of six children, 3 boys & 3 girls. We don't always get along or even speak to each other but there are some things that occur where the need to communicate is of the utmost importance. My younger sister & I are both RN's.

On the evening of <u>December 15</u> I received a phone call from my mom, she said she was having trouble breathing. I found out at that time she had fallen during the week. I encouraged her to go to the ER but she refused & wanted to see her own MD in the morning. Upon seeing her MD she was immediately sent to the Hospital & admitted with pneumonia & difficulty breathing. By that afternoon she was in the ICU with a large blood clot in the area between her lung & chest wall, pneumonia & fluid in the lung. She needed to have a tube placed in to the space to try & clear it. The doctors wanted to give her medication in the chest tube to help break up the blood clot. The medication was agreed upon & begun. The doctors explained that the medication causes a great deal of pain when breaking up the clot. My mother began having more difficulty breathing to the point that they wanted to put a tube down into her airway helping her breathe by using a ventilator. My sister & I discussed this with each other & then our siblings. Mom was placed in a medically induced coma so she couldn't fight the machine. One of us stayed at Mom's bedside day & night. Every morning an ultrasound was done & the clot & other problems were addressed. The doctors kept us well informed of Mom's progress & answered all of our questions. One problem lead to another problem, went into renal failure & we had to make life & death decisions. Although my sister & I are her health care proxy's we never made any decisions that were not agreed upon by all six of us.

The morning of Christmas Day the breathing tube was removed. Mom was breathing on her own but still asleep. After having dinner with my husband & daughter we went out to the hospital. Mom was not doing well; she was having more difficulty breathing. Although one of my sisters were with her & alerting the staff to her needs the doctors were busy elsewhere on the unit. I immediately insisted on seeing the doctor or nursing supervisor as I felt it was unacceptable to watch my mom deteriorate each hour that passed. The doctor came & apologized saying he was unaware of the situation. I ended up staying the night at the hospital. By morning mom was put back on the ventilator. The next thing that was found was as the blood clot problem was resolved the lung itself adhered to the chest wall. Yes mom had to go for surgery to have it separated, like removing a scab from a wound. She remained on the ventilator with the sedation meds although lower doses. Every day we tried to wake her to no avail. When she was finally able to tolerate being off the ventilator the breathing tube was removed. We were concerned she still wasn't waking up. They did a CT scan & found the tiniest stroke, which the neurologist said was so small she would have no deficits from it. Finally in late January mom began waking up a little at a time. By January 21 mom was transferred to a regular room & was sent to a rehab facility three days later. Way too soon we felt for someone who had been so sick for so long. We were told if she didn't go then she would lose the bed so off she went.

Mom was not nearly herself while in rehab, confused, agitated, not eating, wanting no part of the therapy. The therapists took the attitude that they couldn't force her to do the therapy. Most of my siblings & I met with the rehab facility staff & stressed to them it was unacceptable to let her not do her exercises. She went to the hospital, walking & driving & we expected her to be able to walk out!

On March 20, while on a much-needed respite in Florida with my husband I received a phone call from my sister that mom was readmitted to the hospital in critical condition. Mom was found to have a urinary tract infection, the flu, and pneumonia in both lungs & strep in her blood. My sister was not sure mom would make it through the night. My brother was called to come up from Kentucky & told to bring a suit as I caught an earlier flight home from my little trip. Mom was in an isolation room because of the flu. We had all had flu shots but we saw how well that worked with mom having had received one herself. Well mom recovered from all those problems &

was sent to another rehab center. We didn't want her going back to the one where she had gotten so sick.

This time in rehab she was more herself. She worked hard at getting up & learning to walk again. We were encouraged to come see her in the therapy room as they walked her & we encouraged her like a child just a little further mom, come on you can do it & with Help of God & my Father, her Guardian Angel she did it! Being so sick for so long & not being helped to the bathroom when needed incontinence became a problem. Something to be worked on at home. One of my brothers offered to have my mom stay with him for the first week she was home. On May 24, 2014 my mom walked out of rehab & into my brothers house with some help & her walker. I went to help when my work schedule allowed. Therapy came to her house & worked with her. I went down weekly & took her places. Her incontinence went away as she was able to retrain her bladder & get to the bathroom on her own. On May 30, 2014 Mom turned 80 years old. We were skeptical we would ever see the achievement of that milestone but we did.

Now mom walks with a cane! She and one of my sisters recently accompanied me on a trip to Lancaster Pa for the Whoopie Pie Book Club gathering. Another accomplishment! As she was healing & feeling like she'd never get to do things she enjoyed anymore, I believed my encouraging her to work hard so she could go on this trip helped a great deal. Mom, my sister & I had a wonderful time

63

with my Whoopie Pie friends from our first gathering & the new friends I've made this year. Mom was the first one out of her seat when our bus tour arrived at a destination. Mom learned what her new capabilities were & had a taste of things she used to enjoy doing. Now she is back at her senior meeting, looking forward to their little trips & making us crazy because she wants to drive! Anything is possible when everyone pulls together &

I'm grateful to God for My Miracle Mom!

*And he said, The things which are impossible with men are possible with God.*
*Luke 18:27 (KJV)*

## Chocolate Whoopie Pies

*Contest Entry of Mary Ann Schrock*

- 1 1/2 cups lard
- 3 cups white sugar
- 3 eggs
- 3 teaspoons vanilla
- 1 1/2 cups sour milk
- 1 1/2 cups Dutch cocoa
- 3 teaspoons salt
- 6 cups white flour
- 1 1/2 cups hot water
- 3 teaspoons baking soda

Cream together lard and sugar.
Add eggs, beat well.
Add sour milk and vanilla, beating well.
Mix together flour, cocoa and salt.
Dissolve soda in hot water.
Add flour mixture and hot water mixture alternately, beating well after each addition, ending with some of the hot water mixture.
Using number 50 food portioner drop onto ungreased cookie sheet.
Bake at 375° F for 10-12 minutes.

*Fill with Vanilla Filling

### Vanilla Filling

- 3 egg whites
- 3 teaspoons vanilla
- 1/8 teaspoon salt
- 3 tablespoons flour
- 3 tablespoons milk
- 4 cups powdered sugar
- 1 1/2 cups Crisco

Beat egg whites until stiff.
Add vanilla, salt, flour, milk and beat well.
Add powdered sugar and beat well.
Add Crisco and beat until fluffy.
Spread thickly onto a cookie, put another cookie on top and presto!  Whoopie Pie.

**Co-Co Scotchy Whoopie Pies**

*Contest Entry of Karen Phillips*

- 1 cup shortening
- 2 cups sugar
- 2 eggs
- 2 teaspoons vanilla
- 1 cup sour milk
- Cream together
- 2 teaspoons baking soda
- 1 cup hot water
- Mix together
- 4 cups all purpose flour
- 1/2 cup unsweetened cocoa
- 1/2 cup semi-sweet cocoa
- 1/2 cup ground macadamia nuts
- 1 teaspoon salt
- 2 teaspoons cappuccino mix

Preheat oven to 400° F - grease cookie sheet- Cream together first 5 ingredients in a large bowl- combine dry ingredients and add to bowl- stir together baking soda and hot water and add to bowl- drop by tablespoonful onto prepared cookie sheets- bake for 8 minutes in preheated oven until firm but not over baked- cool on baking sheets and transfer to wire racks to cool completely.

*Fill with Butterscotch Filling

**Butterscotch Filling:**

- 6 tablespoons marshmallow cream
- 6 tablespoons butterscotch syrup
- 6 pieces bacon crumbled

Combine and spread on bottom cookie
Decorate if wanted

## Coconut Expresso Whoopie Pies

*Contest Entry of Rachel R. Miller*

- 4 cups flour
- 1 3/4 cups white sugar
- 2 teaspoons baking soda
- 1/2 teaspoons salt
- 1 cup butter
- 1 cup cocoa
- 2 eggs
- 2 teaspoons vanilla
- 1 cup milk
- 1 teaspoon vinegar
- 1/2 cup cold water
- 3 tablespoons instant coffee

Cream together sugar, salt, butter, vanilla and eggs. Combine flour, soda and cocoa. Add to first mixture alternately with the water and milk. Bake at 400° F.

Note: put vinegar in milk and let stand till thick.

*Fill with Coconut Espresso Filling

## Coconut Espresso Filling

- 1 cup Crisco
- 1/2 teaspoon salt
- 1 1/2 tablespoons milk with 2 teaspoons instant coffee
- 4 cups powdered sugar
- 4 ounce cream cheese
- 2 teaspoons coconut extract

Mix in bosch until creamy.
Note: Toast 3/4 cup coconut in oven stirring often and roll cookie into coconut sideways after filled so that it will stick to filling around the edge.
Drizzle with melted chocolate.

## Cranberry White Chip Whoopie Pies

*Best Texture, Taste & Appearance Winner*
*Contest Entry of Dena Schrock*

- 1 cup white sugar
- 1 egg
- 3/4 cup brown sugar
- 1/2 cup butter
- 1 teaspoon baking powder
- 1/4 teaspoon baking soda
- 1/2 teaspoon salt
- 2 tablespoons orange juice
- 1/4 cup milk
- 2 cups flour
- 1/2 cup each of dried cranberries, pecans and vanilla chips

Cream together butter, sugars and egg.
Mix dry ingredients alternately with orange juice and milk.
Bake at 350° F till set. Do not over bake.

*Fill with Buttercream Icing.

### Buttercream Icing

- 1/2 cup butter, softened
- 1/2 cup white Crisco
- 1 tablespoon vanilla
- 4 cups powdered sugar
- enough milk to make right consistency

Mix all ingredients together and spread between two cookies

## Debbie Cookies

*Contest Entry of Fran Miller*

- 2 1/4 cups butter
- 4 1/2 cups brown sugar
- 6 eggs
- 3 teaspoons vanilla
- 3 teaspoons cinnamon
- 2 1/4 teaspoons soda
- 1 1/2 teaspoons salt
- 5 3/4 cups flour
- 6 cups quick oats

Mix in order given.
Bake at 350° F for 8 minutes.


*Fill with Debbie Filling

**Debbie Filling**

- 4 egg whites
- 4 teaspoons vanilla
- 8 tablespoons flour
- 4 tablespoons milk
- 3 cups shortening
- 6 cups powdered sugar

Beat egg whites until stiff peaks, add vanilla, flour and milk and beat well.
Add shortening and powdered sugar and beat for 10 minutes.

## Double Buttermilk Whoopie Pies

*Contest Entry of Mrs. David Elmina Miller*

- 1 1/2 cups white sugar
- 1/2 cup butter
- 2 eggs
- 1 teaspoon vanilla
- 1/2 teaspoon salt
- 1/2 cup baking cocoa
- 1/2 cup hot water
- 1/2 cup buttermilk
- 3 1/2 cups Thesco bread flour
- 1 teaspoon baking soda
- 1 teaspoon baking powder

Cream sugar and butter.
Add eggs and vanilla.
Mix hot water and cocoa together, then add to sugar mixture.
Next add buttermilk.
Beat on low, then add dry ingredients.
Bake at 350° F 10-12 minutes.

*Fill with Peanut Butter Filling

### Peanut Butter Filling

- 1/2 cup peanut butter
- 1/2 cup marshmallow topping
- 1/2 cup milk
- 1 teaspoon vanilla
- 3 cups powdered sugar

Put everything in a bowl and beat till fluffy
Note:  There's no shortening in this filling... very soft and creamy.


*Top with Chocolate Coating


## Chocolate Coating

2 pound coating melted in oven at 375° F for 10-15 minutes.
Put wax paper on cookie sheet and then dip Whoopie pies till coated.
Flip on cookie sheet and chill before handling so chocolate can set.

## Double Mint Whoopie Pies

*Contest Entry of Danielle Feldner*

- 2 1/4 cups flour
- 1 teaspoon baking soda
- 1/2 teaspoon baking powder
- 1/2 teaspoon salt
- 1 cup sugar
- 1/2 cup vegetable shortening
- 1 large egg
- 1 teaspoon mint extract
- 1/2 teaspoon vanilla
- 1/2 cup yogurt
- 1/2 cup hot tea or coffee
- 30 drops green food coloring
- 1/3 cup chopped white and chocolate chips

Preheat oven to 350° F and grease several baking sheets.

Sift together flour, soda, baking powder and salt.

In another bowl beat sugar and shortening until fluffy, then add egg and mint and vanilla and blend thoroughly.

Add half of flour mixture with half of yogurt and tea.

Repeat with remaining halves beating until smooth.

Scoop onto baking sheets with a medium cookie scoop about 2 inches apart.

Bake cookies about 10 minutes. Cool.

Makes 14 Whoopie pies


*Fill with Double Mint Filling

### Double Mint Filling

- 1/2 cup butter
- 1/4 cup vegetable shortening
- 1 1/2 cups powdered sugar or more as needed
- 3 tablespoons marshmallow fluff
- 1 egg white
- 1 tablespoon white chocolate syrup
- 1 tablespoon vanilla
- Pinch of salt
- 2 crushed candy canes

Combine shortening, butter, powdered sugar, marshmallow fluff, egg white, chocolate syrup, vanilla and salt.
Beat until smooth.
Spread half the cookie bottoms with filling and sandwich them together with another cookie.

## Gingerbread Farm Cookies with Hazelnut Icing

*Contest Entry of Rachel Keim*

- 4 cups all purpose flour
- 2 teaspoons ground ginger
- 1 teaspoon baking soda
- 1 teaspoon cinnamon
- 2 tablespoons vinegar
- 1/4 teaspoon salt
- 3/4 cup shortening
- 1 cup brown sugar
- 1 egg
- 1/2 cup molasses

Mix dry ingredients.
In another bowl beat shortening and sugar.
Add egg, molasses and vinegar beating well.
Gradually add to dry ingredients and blend well.
Roll thick. Cut out with cookie cutter.
Bake 375° F for 5-10 minutes.

*Fill with Hazelnut Buttercream Icing.

### Hazelnut Buttercream Icing

- 1/2 cup butter
- 1/2 cup shortening
- 1 teaspoon hazelnut flavoring syrup
- 4 cups powdered sugar
- 2 tablespoons milk

Mix butter and shortening and add flavoring.
Add powdered sugar, one cup at a time and add milk.
Beat on high speed until fluffy, about 5 minutes.

### Grandma Sadie and I by Debbie Curto

Family ties are the ties that stay bound together even when the person has gone to be with Jesus.

My grandmother Sadie is the family member that I feel has the strongest tie to my heart.

The earliest memory I have is grandma and grandpa Joe at their farm (they did not own it but they lived on it and managed it for the owners). I remember the pigs chasing me one day and that was a trauma for a little girl of about four years of age. Grandma and grandpa saved the day by rounding up the pigs and putting them back in the pigpen.

The next memory is of going to the Moon's Laundry and Dry Cleaning (which is now closed) at 5:30 am, because that is where grandma worked. I loved doing that, and yes I know, I was not the typical young girl. I can't go inside a laundry mat without the smell reminding me that I want to be that little girl trailing after Grandma Sadie again and begging her to let me clean out the lint from the dryer drawers. I even liked helping her mop the floors with those heavy mops when she worked the night shift and closed the laundromat. Grandma even did other peoples laundry for them and I loved helping her with the folding of clean clothes. I remember her saying, "You didn't fold that the right way, redo it." I could write forever of the impact and life lessons that the laundromat and grandma made in a lonely young girl's life. Yes Grandma Sadie was a great "life Saver" to me.

I remember Grandma Sadie taking me to church every Sunday and making sure she read her Bible every morning! It was because of her dedication to God that I was saved when I was nine at her little country church.

I took my first and only plane trip with her. It was to Florida to visit my aunt and uncle. I don't remember how old I was but I remember after getting off the plane and walking out of the gated area, a man came up to me, grabbed me and said "that is far enough." I was really scared and started looking around for grandma and then I saw her and she was smiling and I knew then it was my Uncle Bill. I had only seen him once when I was really little so I didn't remember him. I loved the time we spent in Florida and I wish I could visit with Grandma and Uncle Bill and Aunt Sue one more time, but I know I will see them all in Heaven one day.

The one wedding gift I remember receiving is a red and white-checkered bedspread she made for us. It is now in the storage truck, and though it isn't a treasure by any means to anyone but me, it is one of my most treasured heirlooms.

Grandma loved poems and I believe I have gotten my love of poems from her. I have all of her poems she collected and someday, I will go through them and put them in a book and pass them down to one of my grandkids.

I remember Grandma always making us set down in a

chair for about 2 minutes if we started to leave and remember that we forgot something. I have never figured out the reason for that, but it was a part of my childhood, I have never forgotten. I remember her praying for traveling mercies and saying, "Call me when you get home so I know you made it okay" every time we left. I now do the same when my family leaves after visiting us.

I remember Grandma collecting salt & peppershakers. She made me feel special and especially honored because I was the only " kid" she trusted to dust all of her over 1200 sets. I cannot see salt & pepper shakers (of course I'm not talking about the Tupperware and plain sets) without remembering her and the trust she had in me.

I was with her every chance that I got. I went every weekend, every summer, and every holiday. Grandma made sacrifices to be with me: she gave up her time, money, and gas to pick me up (we lived in a different town than her), and her own comfort to make sure I knew she loved me. Even after I was married and had children of mine own, we spent weeks with Grandma Sadie.

Grandma and I always played scrabble. We even played up to the week she died, which she still won most of the time, so you can see where I got my love of words ( her and my mom were both big readers). She would never let me win, because I needed to learn to play the game the right way.

Grandma always made me Cherry pie for my birthday,

and I think of her every time I see a Cherry Pie. She always told others they could have a piece after I got the first piece. She also made homemade noodles, I can still see her brown round pan with noodles laying on it and yes, I always tried to eat them before they were done drying out and before they were cooked.

I am so grateful that I was able to tell Grandma Sadie that I loved her before she died! I remember getting that phone call while grocery shopping that grandma had went into a coma, and rushing to the hospital and meeting my sister Tonja coming out of the elevator, who told me Grandma just woke up. So I went to her room and said, "Grandma I love you and it's ok with me if you want to Go Home to Jesus and Grandpa. I will miss you and always love you but I don't want you to suffer anymore, and it is time." It was the hardest thing I have ever done, but I believe it was the thing to do. She died that night, peacefully in her sleep.

I remember praying all the way to that hospital, about a 45 minute drive, " Let me tell her once more " I Love You" and I am so thankful that God allowed me to do so!

When my family found out that I was writing about Grandma Sadie, they wanted to add their thoughts, so I am adding them here so you can see that we all felt that Grandma Sadie was a wonderful lady. They are not in any particular order, I just typed them as I received them.

Carl (my husband):  Grandma was a special person. I

remember taking her to the cemeteries each Memorial Day. I remember playing Yahtzee and Shanghai Rummy (which Debbie and I taught her to play, (yes she played Yahtzee but we had to convince her that rummy wasn't gambling. I loved her like she was my grandma, which she was.

Teresa (my cousin):

One thing that has always impressed me about Grandma Sadie is that for her time in life, I always appreciated the fact that she was such an independent woman, and that she never remarried just to have a man around. She was always firm, but kind at the same time. She reminded me a lot of my dad, and I know how much he loved her.

Mom:

She loved to help others and she took older people who didn't drive to the store, church and other places they needed to go. She showed her love to her family every day.

Lou (my sister):

I loved her so much. She told me once to wear purple because it's for royalty.....but I shouldn't wear red cause people would call me Mrs. Claus. We both laughed. And the thing I remember the most is that she loved people and her Christian morals and her prayers.

Joe (my son):

I remember Grandma as being a Cubs fan and the rest of us being Cardinals fans and when they played against each other and the Cubs or the Cardinals got a great hit or made a great play, she would cheer for that team. We asked her why she was cheering and clapping for the Cardinals, she would reply "Just because I'm for the other team doesn't mean I can't applaud for the team that does good. We all need to know when we done good, there is too much negativity in this world already."

Tonja (my sister):

She used to make awesome blackberry cobbler. When we would get together for a family thing, she would always try to make some for me.

Sandra (my niece):

I remember when grandma was in the nursing home she couldn't or never really called anyone by their actual names, but she remembered my name and mom's name. Towards the end, mom and I were the only ones that could feed her as she wouldn't let anyone, not even the cnas or any other family members ...I love and miss her. I made a birthday cake for her this year: 104 ! She's missed a lot !!!

(Me adding to this): She did remember my name but I didn't try to feed her.

Grandma Sadie passed away on April 19, 2002, 18 days before her 92nd Birthday. My family ties with her will never be broken. I want to close this memoir by saying, " I love and miss Grandma Sadie every day and it feels like she is still here with me in my heart."

And I also want to include this poem I found on the Internet. I didn't write it, I don't know who did, but it expresses my thoughts perfectly.

Grandma
Author Unknown

A baby cradled in your arms...
Teaching me your gentle charms.
Growing up with you by my side...
Learning from you never to lie.
To understand and not judge too...
Love and kindness I also learned from you.
Through the years you watched me grow...
Teaching me everything I'd need to know.
Listening to every word I've said...
And every word I've wrote you've read.
You've been there for me to the end...
Until the day for you, God did send.
Now you watch me from up above...
Shining down on me your heavenly love.
I will miss you with all my heart...
Thank you for being there from the start.

### Jennifer's Banana Pudding Whoopie Pie

*Contest Entry of Jennifer Biddle*

- 1 cup (2 sticks) unsalted butter, room temperature
- 2 cups sifted powder sugar
- 1 1/2 ounces sifted powder sugar
- 7 1/2 ounces marshmallow fluff
- 2 teaspoons vanilla
- 1/2 cup plus 2 teaspoon oil
- 1 cup water
- 1-3.4 ounce box instant banana pudding
- 1-3.4 ounce box instant vanilla pudding
- 4 eggs
- 1 box vanilla wafers
- 1 box vanilla cake

In a big bowl combine cake mix, oil, water, eggs and both boxes of pudding.
Mix together until creamy.
Spoon batter into a Whoopie pie baking pan about half full.
Bake at 350° F for 10 minutes.

### Filling directions

Cream butter and sugar until pale and fluffy. Then add marshmallow and vanilla. Mix on low for 3 minutes. Using a heaping spoon place the filling on the bottom of one of the cakes spreading until desired thickness. Crumble vanilla wafer cookies on top of the filling and then place another cake on top and sprinkle with powdered sugar and a few cookie crumbs.

## Lemon Snowflake Whoopie Pies

*Contest Entry of Dena Schrock*

- 1 cup butter
- 1 1/2 cups white sugar
- 2 eggs
- 2 teaspoons baking soda
- 2 teaspoons baking powder
- 2 teaspoons cream of tartar
- 4 cups flour
- 1 cup milk
- 1 teaspoon vanilla

Cream together first 3 ingredients alternating dry ingredients and milk.
Bake at 350° F for 8-10 minutes or until done.

*Fill with lemon icing.

**Lemon Filling**

- 4 tablespoons butter, softened
- 2 cups powdered sugar
- Juice from 2 lemons or enough juice to make the right consistency.

Decorate with edible glitter and sparkling white sugar if desired.

**Owl Whoopie Pies**

*Most Creative Winner ~*
*Contest Entry of Sue Gibson*

- 1 2/3 cups flour
- 2/3 cup cocoa
- 1'1/2 teaspoon soda
- Pinch salt
- Sift together
- 4 tablespoons soft butter
- 4 tablespoons Crisco
- 1 cup light brown sugar
- Beat in mixer
- 1 egg
- 1 teaspoon vanilla
- Beat egg and vanilla
- 1 cup milk.

Preheat oven to 375° F.
Sift together flour, cocoa, soda and salt
Beat in mixer: butter, Crisco and sugar.
Gradually add milk and flour mixture til completely mixed.
Drop scoop of batter on cookie sheets.
Bake 10 minutes. Makes 8 full pies
For wings- melt peanut butter in microwave. Put in squeeze bottle and decorate.

**Peanut Butter Frosting**

- 2 cups powdered sugar
- 1/4 cup milk
- 1/4 cup butter
- 1/2 cup peanut butter
- 2 teaspoons vanilla

Mix all together with mixer and put scoop between Whoopie pies.

**Chocolate Sugar Glaze**

- 1 1/2 cups powdered sugar
- 4-5 tablespoons hot water
- 3 tablespoons cocoa

Mix in pan on stove till thickened a little.
Pour over 8 of the pies.
Add embellishments.

### Pecan Maple Syrup Whoopie Pies

*Contest Entry of Esta Borntrager*

- 1/2 cup plus 3 tablespoons butter, softened
- 3/4 cup brown sugar
- 1 large egg
- 2 1/2 cups all purpose flour
- 2 1/2 teaspoons baking powder
- Pinch of salt
- 2/3 cup maple syrup
- 1/4 cup milk
- 1 teaspoon vanilla
- 1 cup pecans

Mix together butter, sugar and vanilla till fluffy.
Add eggs and beat again, adding baking powder, salt,
maple syrup, flour and milk.
Add nuts.
Bake at 350° F.

*Fill with buttercream icing.

**Buttercream Icing Filling**

- 1 1/4 cups milk
- 5 tablespoons flour
- pinch of salt.

Boil ingredients until thick.   Cool.

Part 2
- 1 cup Crisco
- 1/2 cup butter
- 1 cup sugar
- 1 teaspoon vanilla

Beat together Crisco and butter till creamy.
Add sugar and beat again.
Then add part one and beat till light and fluffy.

### Pumpkin Whoopie Pies

*Contest Entry of Esta Borntrager*

- 3 cups flour
- 1 tablespoon cinnamon &'pumpkin spice
- 1 teaspoon baking powder
- 1 teaspoon baking soda
- 1 cup white sugar
- 1 cup brown sugar
- 1 cup vegetable oil
- 15 ounces pumpkin
- 1 teaspoon vanilla
- 2 eggs

Mix oil, sugar and eggs.
Add soda, baking powder and spices. Mix well.
Add pumpkin and flour.
Bake at 350° F.

### Caramel Filling

- 1/2 cup butter
- 1 cup brown sugar
- 1/3 cup condensed milk or sour cream

Melt butter, add sugar till mixed.
Add liquid and boil for 1 minute.
Cool and add powdered sugar till right consistency.

## Pumpkin Whoopie Pies

*Contest Entry of Katherine Miller*

- 2 cups brown sugar
- 1 cup vegetable oil
- 1 1/2 cups pumpkin
- 3 cups flour
- 2 eggs
- 1 teaspoon salt
- 1 teaspoon baking powder
- 1 teaspoon soda
- 2 tablespoon pumpkin pie spice
- 1 teaspoon vanilla
- 1 tablespoon lemon juice

Cream oil and sugar.
Add pumpkin, eggs and dry ingredients.
Drop by large tablespoons on cookie sheet.
Bake at 350° F.

**Vanilla Filling**

- 1 teaspoon vanilla
- 1-8 ounce cream cheese
- 4 tablespoons butter
- 5 cups powdered sugar
- 1-7 ounce marshmallow cream

Cream butter and cream cheese.
Add vanilla and powdered sugar.  Mix well.
Add marshmallow cream. Enjoy!

**My Family Ties by Kathy Milburn**

When I was a very small girl, my parents always took us 6 children to visit my Grandparents on Sundays where we always had a big dinner. Even though I was so very young, I can remember it like it was yesterday. My mother would always dress me in a frilly dress, ruffled socks, and even ruffles on my underwear! Patent leather shoes, too, ya know, the shiny fake leather type. My mom and dad had 6 children and, although my dad worked at the steel mill, making little money, they always took care of us. My mom didn't work, always thought she was a mother and it was her place to be home taking care of the house and us kids.

Back to my grandparents house, my father's parents. When we would go there, my dad's only brother, his wife and their daughter (my cousin) would be there as well. My cousin, and I shared the same name. So when anyone would call out "our" name, we would both go running to them. I can remember when this happened once, we collided into one another, both falling and getting dirty. My mother shook it off and said it was okay, you'll wash and so will your dress. BUT now my cousin...Her parents were SO upset, they yelled at me for pushing her down. Why me, I thought. When I told my mom what happened, she told me... things happen while playing.

You'll wash and I will get your dress all washed up and

pretty again...that made me smile even though the rest of the day, I couldn't play with my cousin., Her parents made her sit next to them and she wasn't allowed to play anymore.

We enjoyed dinners at my grandparents' home for many years, even as they started to age. When my grandfather passed away, my grandmother still had a few more years of Sunday dinners. After it became too much for my grandmother to handle anymore, my mom started having her own family dinners at her house. That went on for a lot of years, until my father passed away at an early age of 56. At that time, all 5 of my brothers were married with families of their own. So my mother decided to stop having the Sunday dinners at her home.

Shortly after my father passed away, all of us children thought it would be better for my mom to sell the house and get an apartment. We would all feel better having our mom in a safe place that she was capable of caring for. My parents' house was too big for just my mother, and the 5 acres of ground was too much for her to care for, too. Between a few of her children, we would take turns going there and mowing the lawn, about 2 of the 5 acres.

Finally, were able to talk her into moving into an apartment, and she was happy, as well as all us kids, too. With my godmother living across the parking lot from her, that made it a lot better for her also, she was bored and always alone. Because all of us kids had jobs and other things going on in our lives as well, it was just too hard to see mom everyday like she wanted. But, even if we weren't there on a daily basis, we would always call her every day.

I had 3 children of my own by then, and they didn't always want to leave their friends to go visit grandma. So, I would ask my mother to come spend a few nights with us. She and my brothers knew that if they wanted to visit with her, they were always welcome to come to my house. So,

Mom started coming and staying at my house more frequently, and if we needed to go somewhere the kids didn't want to go, my mom would tell us to leave them home and she would watch them. As time went on, she would stay for weeks on end.

She was just happy to have someone around her all the time and would call me, asking if she could come spend time at my house...I would go get her, as she didn't drive and she would stay a few weeks at a time.

Then one day I had to go away to Maine on a trip, and knowing this, she told me not to get

Someone else to watch my kids, she would just come and stay, get them all off to school and take care of them. I would call home while away, checking on her and seeing how the kids were, and she would tell me everything was just fine and not to worry about rushing home. It was November, icy and snowy in Maine. Terrible weather we had to travel through to get home to Ohio. When I got home, at the back door stood my daughter who was 9 years old at the time, and my oldest son who was 15. Shocked, I looked at them wondering why they weren't in school. So when I got into the house, I asked...where is grandma and your brother, who was 12 years old. My son started crying and said I had to call Uncle Joe at the ER, it's something about grandma, she had a hard time breathing and his brother went with grandma in the ambulance. I started freaking out, and told the kids to get in the car: we were going to the hospital to see what was wrong with grandma. When we walked in the ER, I saw some of my family crying but I still didn't know what was going on with my mom. I asked my sister in law, and she told me that I had to go into this one room where the rest of my family was at that time. Upon entering the room, I was told my mother had passed away. Oh Lord...I about lost it, running through the halls yelling where is my mother...They took me to the room she was in, ONLY after I calmed down, and I finally got to see my mother. Then I about passed out.

So, my story started out so-so, and then went to pieces in the end. I have neither parent, just 5 older brothers, no sisters... Now I have 4 brothers as my oldest brother passed away last year. No matter what, I stay close to all my brothers now! We had only 1 aunt who was like our second mother, but she passed away last year, too!

I will always remember the good times from when I was little, and all of the good times I've had growing up in my family. That's something I will always treasure.

Never take anything for granted because you never know when it will not be there anymore to enjoy!

God Bless

*I can do all things through Christ*
*which strengtheneth me.*
*Phillipians 4:13 (KJV)*

## Pumpkin Whoopie Pies

*Contest Entry of Esther Raber*

- 1 cup Crisco
- 2 cups brown sugar
- 2 eggs
- 2 cups pumpkin, cooked
- 1 teaspoon vanilla
- 1/2 teaspoon ginger
- 1/2 teaspoon cloves
- 1 teaspoon baking soda
- 1 teaspoon salt
- 1 teaspoon baking powder

Preheat oven to 375° F.
Cream shortening, then add sugar, eggs, pumpkin and vanilla.
Add dry ingredients.
Bake for 10 minutes.

*Fill with Vanilla Icing

**Vanilla Icing**

- 1 egg white
- 2 tablespoons milk
- 3/4 cup Crisco
- 2 tablespoons flour
- 1 teaspoon vanilla
- 4 1/2 cup powdered sugar

Beat egg white, milk and Crisco.
Then add flour, vanilla and powdered sugar.
Beat until fluffy.

## Pumpkin Whoopie Pies

*Contest Entry of Betty Yoder*

- 1 3/4 cup brown sugar
- 1 cup vegetable oil
- 1 1/2 cup pumpkin
- 2 eggs
- 3 cups flour
- 1 teaspoon baking powder
- 1 teaspoon soda
- 1 teaspoon vanilla
- 1 teaspoon salt
- 1 1/2 teaspoon cinnamon

Cream sugar and oil.
Add eggs, pumpkin and vanilla.  Blend well.
Add sifted dry ingredients and mix well.
By using your cookie dropper drop dough on hot waffle iron.
Bake at 350° F until browned only 2-4 minutes.

### Vanilla Filling

- 3 ounces cream cheese
- 1/4 cup butter
- 1/2 teaspoon vanilla
- 3 cups powdered sugar

Mix all ingredients.
Spread between cookies.
Yields 2-2 1/2 dozen depending on your size cookie dropper.
Can easily be frozen.

### Pumpkin Whoopie Pies

*Contest Entry of Mary Esta Yoder*

- 1 cup vegetable oil
- 2 cups brown sugar
- 1 1/2 cups solid pack pumpkin
- 2 eggs
- 1 teaspoon vanilla
- 3 cups flour
- 1 teaspoon salt
- 1 teaspoon soda
- 1 teaspoon baking powder
- 1 teaspoon cinnamon
- 1 teaspoon pumpkin pie spice

Beat together first 4 ingredients.
Sift dry ingredients and add to first 4 ingredients.
Drop onto hot waffle iron.
Bake 2-3 minutes till done. Cool.

*Fill with Cream Cheese Filling

### Cream Cheese Filling

- 4 ounces cream cheese
- 1/4 cup butter
- 1/2 teaspoon vanilla
- 3 cups powdered sugar

Put 2 cookies together with a dollop of cream cheese filling.

### Samoa Whoopies

*Contest Entry of Fran Miller*

- 1 2/3 cups all-purpose flour
- 2/3 cup unsweetened cocoa powder
- 1 1/2 teaspoons baking soda
- 1/2 teaspoon salt
- 4 tablespoons unsalted butter, softened
- 4 tablespoons vegetable shortening
- 1 cup packed dark brown sugar
- 1 egg
- 1 teaspoon vanilla
- 1 cup milk
- 1 teaspoon coconut extract (optional)

Preheat oven to 350° F.

Line baking sheets with parchment paper.

In a bowl sift together flour, cocoa, baking soda and salt.

In another bowl beat butter, shortening and sugar with a mixer on low until just combined.

Increase speed to medium and beat for about 3 minutes. Add egg, vanilla and coconut extract. Beat for 2 more minutes.

Add half of the flour mixture and half of the milk and beat on low until incorporated. Repeat with remaining flour and milk and beat until combined.

Using a tablespoon drop batter on baking sheet two inches apart. Bake for about 10 minutes each or until pies spring back when pressed gently.

Remove from oven and cool about 5 minutes before transferring them to a rack to cool completely.

*Fill with Caramel Buttercream Frosting

### Caramel Buttercream Frosting

- 2 sticks unsalted butter
- 1/2 teaspoon salt
- 3/4 cup packed brown sugar
- 2 teaspoons vanilla
- 1/3 cup prepared caramel
- 3 tablespoons milk
- 6 cups powdered sugar
- 1 cup sweetened shredded coconut
- 1/4 cup milk chocolate chips

Cream butter and brown sugar together in a bowl of an electric or stand mixer.
Add vanilla, salt, caramel syrup, milk until combined.
Begin adding in the sugar slowly and mixing thoroughly after each addition.
Beat for about 4 minutes or until smooth.
To toast the coconut spread the coconut onto a rimmed baking sheet.
Toast in oven at 350° F stirring frequently until the coconut is an even brown color about 10 minutes.
Heat chocolate chips in a double boiler or microwave for about 30 seconds or until drizzling consistency.
Spoon the caramel butter cream into a decorators bag.
Pipe caramel butter cream out onto Whoopie Pie.
Top with toasted coconut.
Drizzle chocolate over coconut and immediately sandwich between two pies before chocolate sets.
For added coconut you may roll the sides in Flaked coconut.

## Spiced Orange and Cranberry Whoopie Pies

*Contest Entry of Linda C. Scott*

- 3 cup sun sifted cake flour
- 1 teaspoon baking soda
- 1 teaspoon baking powder
- 4 teaspoons ground nutmeg
- 2 teaspoons ground ginger
- 1 teaspoon ground cloves
- 1 1/2 teaspoons salt
- 2 sticks butter
- 2 cups packed dark brown sugar
- 4 large egg
- 2 teaspoons vanilla
- 1-6 ounce container Chobani Blood Orange Greek Yogurt
- 1 orange (to make 3-4 teaspoons grated zest and 1/4 cup juice)
- 1 1/2 cup Craisins

Preheat oven to 350° F.

In a large bowl of an electric mixer, beat together the butter and sugar.

Add eggs one at a time, beating after each one until well combined.

Add the vanilla and beat again.

In a separate bowl, combine all of the dry ingredients and blend together.

Add 1/2 of the dry ingredients into the egg mixture and stir together.

Add the yogurt and stir again.

Add remaining dry ingredients and stir again.

Stir in the orange juice and beat well on medium speed with electric mixer until well blended.

Add the Craisins and blend together on low setting.

114

With a 2 teaspoon size cookie scoop, scoop out 80 circles of batter on a ungreased non stick cookie sheet. Bake 10 minutes. Let cool.

Place about 2 teaspoons of the filling on 40 cookies and top with remaining 40 cookies.

Store in airtight container in the refrigerator overnight to maintain freshness and marry the flavors together.

*Fill with Spiced Orange and Cranberry Filling

## Spiced Orange and Cranberry Filling

- ½ cup butter
- ¼ cup Crisco
- 1-8 ounce cream cheese
- 2 pounds powdered sugar
- 3 teaspoons zest from the orange

Cream butter, Crisco and cream cheese together with a electric mixer.
Gradually add powdered sugar.
Whip until light and fluffy.
Add orange zest and mix on low speed.
Spread filling across half of the cooled cookie circles and top with remaining cookie circle.

*And we know that all things work together for good
to them that love God, to them who are the called
according to his purpose.
Romans 8:28 (KJV)*

## Strawberry Filled Whoopie Pies

*Contest Entry of Esta Borntrager*

- 1 box white cake mix
- 1 teaspoon vanilla
- 1/2 teaspoon almond flavoring
- 1/4 cup butter, melted
- 2 large eggs
- 1 1/4 cup buttermilk

Beat first 6 ingredients at low speed till moist.
Increase speed to medium and beat 2 minutes or till
smooth.
Bake at 350° F.

*Fill with strawberry filling.

**Strawberry Filling**

Filling part one. Cook till thick then cool.
- 5 tablespoons flour
- 1 1/4 cup milk
- Pinch salt

Filling part two
- 1 cup Crisco
- 1/2 cup butter
- 1 cup sugar
- 1/3 cup strawberry jam

Mix butter and Crisco till creamy, then beat in sugar till nice and creamy.
Add part one, little at a time till light and fluffy.

## Tropical Chocolate Whoopie Pies

All Organic, Gluten Free and Flourless

*Contest Entry of Kimberly Weils*

- 1 cup black beans
- 3 tablespoons cocoa powder
- 1 egg
- 1 1/2 tablespoons coconut oil
- 1 teaspoon vanilla
- 1/4 cup raw honey
- 1 1/2 teaspoons baking soda
- Pinch of salt

Preheat oven to 350° F.
Process beans in food processor until creamy.
Add cocoa powder, egg, oil, vanilla, honey, baking soda and salt and process until blended.
Fill muffin cups with 2-3 tablespoons of batter.
Bake for 15-20 minutes or until toothpick comes out clean.
Let cool for 30 minutes.


*Fill with Tropical Coconut Filling

### Tropical Coconut Filling

- Coconut cream pudding
- 1 can full fat coconut milk
- 1 large egg
- 3 tablespoons arrowroot powder
- 3 tablespoons raw honey
- 1/2 teaspoon vanilla
- 1/2 cup shredded coconut, toasted
- Pinch salt
- 16 ounce cream cheese softened
- 1 cup heavy whipping cream
- 14 ounce can crushed pineapple
- 1 1/2 bananas

Process until smooth and fill pies.

### Turtle Whoopie Pie

*Contest Entry of Mary Ann Conner*

- 1 cup butter
- 2/3 cup sugar
- 1 cup brown sugar
- 2 eggs
- 1 tablespoon vanilla
- 1/4 cup oil
- 1 1/2 cups sour milk
- 4 cups flour
- 1 cup cocoa
- 1 teaspoon salt
- 3 teaspoons baking soda
- 1 teaspoon baking powder

Preheat oven to 375° F (convection oven to 315° F)
In a large electric mixer, add sugars, butter and eggs and beat thoroughly.
Add the oil and vanilla and beat until blended.
In a separate bowl combine the flour, cocoa, baking powder, baking soda and salt to the egg mixture and beat until mixed.
Add the sour milk and beat until mixed.
With a tablespoon scoop dough onto a cookie sheet.
Bake 10-12 minutes. Let cool.

*Fill with Turtle Filling

### Turtle Filling

- 4 tablespoons flour
- 4 tablespoons milk
- 2 teaspoons vanilla
- 3 cups powdered sugar
- 1 1/4 cups Crisco
- 1 1/3 cups marshmallow topping

In a saucepan mix the flour and milk.
While stirring, over medium heat, cook until thickened. Let cool.
Put in an electric mixer bowl and add the vanilla, powdered sugar and Crisco. Mix well.
Add the marshmallow topping and stir to combine.
Spread the filling evenly on one of the Whoopie Pie rounds, then add a second round as a top, continuing until all rounds and filling has been used.

*Top with Turtle Frosting

### Turtle Frosting

- 4 ounces Bakers German Sweet Chocolate
- 1 tablespoon butter
- 3 tablespoons water
- 1 cup sifted confectioners sugar
- Dash of salt
- 1/2 teaspoon vanilla
- Caramel sauce
- Finely chopped walnuts

Combine the chocolate, butter and water in a small saucepan and stir over low heat until blended and smooth.
Combine the sugar and salt in a mixing bowl.
Gradually add the chocolate mixture, blending well.
Add the vanilla. Mix well. Makes 3/4 cup.
Spread the frosting on the completed rounds.
Drizzle caramel sauce over the chocolate frosting.
Sprinkle chopped walnuts lightly over the top of all.

*Jesus said unto him, If thou canst believe, all things are possible to him that believeth.*
*Mark 9:23*

**Pumpkin Whoopie Pies**

*Pumpkin Whoopie Pies with Maple Cream Cheese Filling*
*A favorite of Chris Meyer, Memories by Chris*

- 2 cups all purpose flour
- 1 teaspoon baking powder
- 1 teaspoon baking soda
- 1 teaspoon cinnamon
- 1/4 teaspoon nutmeg
- 1/4 teaspoon ginger
- 1/2 teaspoon salt
- 1/2cup unsalted butter softened
- 1 1/4 cup regular granulated sugar
- 2 large eggs lightly beaten (room temp is always best)
- 1 cup pure pumpkin puree (canned or fresh)
- 1 teaspoon pure vanilla extract

Preheat the oven to 350° F and line baking sheets with parchment paper. Combine flour and dry ingredients in a large mixing bowl. Beat butter and sugar in a mixer and then add eggs slowly while blending on low. Add pumpkin and vanilla and beat on low speed until smooth. Don't over beat. Stir in your flour mixture until combined. I use a small scoop and drop on cookie trays so they are all consistent size. You can use a small scoop for mini whoopie pies or a regular ice cream scoop size for large whoopie pies.
Bake for 10-12 minutes depending on size. They should be a cake like consistency and spring back to the touch.
Cool for a few minutes and transfer to wire racks to cool completely before filling.

*Fill with Maple Cream Cheese Filling

## Maple Cream Cheese filling

- 8 ounces cream cheese, softened and room temperature
- 12 Tablespoon softened unsalted butter
- 1 teaspoon Maple flavoring OR pure Maple Syrup
- 3 cups sifted powdered sugar and a dash of cinnamon for color

For filling ~beat cream cheese, butter and maple until light and fluffy. Sift the powdered sugar and a dash of cinnamon so there are no lumps and gradually beat into your wet mixture. Adjust Maple to taste.

Next! The fun part. Scoop or pipe in filling and top with another cookie to make your finished whoopie pie! I make a generous amount of filling and you may have some left over, but I promise you, that won't last long if you do. Leftover filling makes a nice dip for apple slices or on a toasted bagel!

TIP ~freeze them to make filling much easier! And you can freeze the finished product just as well also! Not that you will need to because I will doubt you will have any leftover to worry about freezing.

**Memories by Chris Photography**

Chris Meyer lives on a 5-acre farm in Kentucky with her husband Bob, 3 dogs, 3 cats, 2 horses, 2 tropical birds, ducks and chickens. She is a full time caregiver to her 94-year-old Grandmother who suffers from dementia. Her husband Bob helps with Granny duty when Chris travels to do any freelance photography assignments.

Chris runs her freelance photography business from home while also journaling her experience of caring for her retired Grandparents for almost 4 years. She writes for a non-profit organization called *Seniors for Pets* based out of Southwest Florida. Chris's work has been featured in the *Kentucky Mountain Saddle Horse Association* and the *Rocky Mountain Horse Association Magazines*. Her food and Amish living photographs have been published in *Cooking & Such Magazine* and also published in a cookbook published by Zondervan.

Chris' time on weekends and evenings is spent doing landscape, equine, portrait and wedding photography. During the day she is often baking and cooking meals for food photography assignments.

Her goal for 2014/2015 is to write a Children's photo book and start a blog about farm life in Kentucky including stories about care taking, recipes, gardening and the joys of living with a barn yard full of animals.

You can contract Chris at
www.facebook.com/memoriesbychris

or email
memoriesbychris@yahoo.com

### Walnut Creek Cheese

Tucked in the heart of Ohio Amish country, Walnut Creek Cheese is a store like no other. Shopping at Walnut Creek Cheese is where it's not just food but fun. In a town of 600, there will be 10,000 to 20,000 customers that will pass through the doors of Walnut Creek Cheese to shop every week.

It all started with a pickup truck and a slide-in refrigerated box in April 1977 when Mark Coblentz, a 21 year old with more spunk than sense filled his truck and began peddling cheese and Trail bologna to retail stores. Coming from conservative Amish Mennonite parents, Mark was taught the importance of honesty and going the extra mile. Honesty and integrity have always been hallmarks of Walnut Creek Cheese.

Today Walnut Creek cheese has two retail stores. The main retail store in Walnut Creek, Ohio and a smaller one in downtown Berlin, Ohio. Walnut Creek Cheese employs 220 associates who have the customer's best interest at heart. Visiting either of these stores is just plain fun!

For the full store and for more information about Walnut Creek Cheese and their other ventures such as Walnut Creek Foods, you can visit their website at www.walnutcreekcheese.com .

## One More Thing...

If you enjoyed this book, I'd be very grateful if you'd post a short review on Amazon. Your support really does make a difference.

If you'd like to leave a review or would like a list of my books, you will find them on Amazon. And don't forget to follow me on Facebook so that you can hear firsthand about new, upcoming releases.

With blessings,

*"Whoopie Pie" Pam*

### About "Whoopie Pie" Pam Jarrell

Author Pamela Jarrell, best known as "Whoopie Pie" Pam, is the author of several wonderful story/cookbooks, and best-selling co-author of the #1 best selling series, The Divine Secrets of the Whoopie Pie Sisters. She is also the founder and creator of the Whoopie Pie Book Club, a well-known social media site.

While battling Papillary Thyroid Carcinoma, Pam created the Whoopie Pie Book Club. For years, she called a group of ladies in her family by that same name. Every year, they travelled to Amish country for a retreat of reading Amish fiction, seeing the Amish sights and eating plenty of Whoopie Pies.

Inspired by the Amish for their simplicity in facing life, love of God, and honor for family, Pam found a connection with the Amish. As a result of her many years of traveling and conducting business with the Amish, she has established close friendships with many Amish families, friendships that she cherishes. She refers to them as her extended family.

She now resides in Florida in a little place she calls Paradise. When not reading, writing or traveling, she spends time with her family of three children, one son-in-law and three awesome grandchildren. The remaining portion of her time is spent interacting with her cherished members of the Whoopie Pie Book Club.

Contact Pam on

Facebook
https://www.facebook.com/whoopiepiepam

Whoopie Pie Book Club
https://www.facebook.com/groups/whoopiepiebookclub/

Visit her Web Blog
http://whoopiepieplace.com

Email
whoopiepieplace@yahoo.com

**Divine Secrets of the Whoopie Pie Sisters**

## Excerpt

## The Dock

Sitting on the dock, a sense of relaxation washed over Leah as she let her eyes wander nonchalantly over the water. It was crystal clear and completely calm, the serene glasslike surface barely marred by the occasional ripple caused by a dragon fly fluttering down to dip its legs into the water, from the edge of a water lily. The sun had already begun its nightly descent over the hill, right behind the Millers' family farm, its orange glow from the perfectly shaped orb casting glittering embers all across the pond. A bird flew overhead, heading toward the woods that bordered the large farm property. It disappeared into the sea of green leaves that clung to the branches, motionless in this breezeless late summer evening.

Leah sighed and returned her attention back to the pond, contemplating that it wouldn't be long before the surface would turn into a crystal sheet of ice. It was only late August and she knew that she shouldn't be already thinking about winter, but she so dreaded that season: cold, grey, dark. *No*, Leah thought to herself. Winter was not her favorite time of year, that was for sure and certain!

But, as her *grossmammi* had always pointed out, "You

have to go through winter before you can get to spring!" *Wise advice from an even wiser woman*, Leah thought. If only *Grossmammi* Maggie was still around. Leah could sure use her advice and her wisdom right now.

Instead, Leah felt alone. Even more than alone; lonely. Whenever such feelings overcame her, feelings of worry and fear, she would escape the craziness of her home, even if only for a few moments, to sit on the dock, her bare feet dipped into the cool water as she reflected on the problems at hand. After all, this pond had always been her favorite spot; her place to find solace and to recapture her spirit. And of late, Leah Mast needed a lot of that.

As she watched two little sparrows play in the branches of a nearby weeping willow, Leah found herself smiling. *That* was a peaceful moment, she reckoned, one that gave her a sense of tranquility after a long and stressful day. Oh, how Leah loved these sparrows, always thinking of the Bible verse that stated God even took care of the little sparrow! They were her favorite bird and observing them always made her realize that there was more to life than met the eye. Watching those little birds flit and flutter through the branches always made her wonder why life couldn't be that simple for humans. Their play was as innocent as that of a newborn baby.

Leah began to shiver. She wasn't sure if it were the cool northern wind that was now blowing an evening chill through her bones or the acknowledgement that her family's lives were a mess. From the day that they each entered the world, Leah had felt a responsibility for her siblings. And more so, two years ago, when their parents were killed in a car accident while on their way to a cousin's wedding in Pennsylvania. Leaving behind the family business, her parents had also left Leah with something else to tend to: their two youngest *kinner[1]*. Even today, that was not easy for a young woman of 34 years who already had her own growing family of seven children.

*How can I hold it together?* She asked herself again, more as a statement than an actual question. Indeed, it was the question that she asked herself every single time she escaped to the pond, just after shutting down the store and before preparing for evening chores. Yet, holding it together was the one thing that Leah was good at doing. After all, she had been given no choice. Her family *needed* her. Of that, she was constantly reminded. Not only was she the oldest, but she had always been considered the strong one: the one that everyone depended upon in a time of crisis; the one her mother had entrusted with her prize bakery: Whoopie Pie Place.

To Leah, this responsibility gave her a great secret. But that secret came with a weight. It gave her pride, something she would never admit among her peers or family. Pride was one thing that Amish people were supposed to avoid. But Leah knew that she was proud of the bakery and of its widespread

---

[1] Children

reputation as *the only place* outside of Berlin, Ohio, where one could purchase authentic Whoopie Pies. People ordered them from all around the country, asking for shipments to arrive in time for birthdays, anniversaries, Christmas and Easter.

Yes, the continued success of the bakery gave Leah great pride. But, at times, it made her bone weary as well.

*Indeed,* she thought as she started to get to her feet, her eyes scanning the horizon. *How long can I hold all of this, the family, the business, and my sanity...together?*

Divine Secrets of the Whoopie Pie Sisters
*by best-selling author of Amish Christian Romances, Sarah Price, and Whoopie Pie Pam Jarrell.*

Follow the story of four Amish sisters who run Whoopie Pie Place, the best-known bakery outside of Berlin, Ohio. Each sister has a secret that influences their lives and, unknowingly, impacts each other. Yet, little by little, the pressure of balancing their responsibilities of their daily lives with their individual secrets becomes harder to manage.

The Divine Secrets of the Whoopie Pie Sisters is a different type of Amish Christian story. By blending Sarah Price's 25 years experience of living among the Amish in Pennsylvania with Pamela Jarrell's extensive 15 years experience interacting and befriending the Amish in Berlin, Ohio, Price and Jarrell team up to give the readers a new type of story that focuses not so much on romance but on friendships and the reality of day-to-day life living among the Amish.

136

*Yea, though I walk through the valley of the shadow of death, I will fear no evil: for thou art with me; thy rod and thy staff they comfort me.*
*Psalms 23:4 (KJV)*